Table of Contents

Table of Contents
Description
Dedication
Prologue
Introduction
Chapter 1 – My Family
Chapter 2 – My Job
Chapter 3 – My Adventures
Chapter 4 – My Challenges
Chapter 5 – My Goals
Epilogue

Description

"Why Am I So Special?" is the autobiography of Barry Henkin, a man whose kind heart, optimistic disposition, and encyclopedic memory for music and faces have enabled him to overcome the physical, mental, emotional, and societal obstacles that have confronted him since birth.

Third Edition © Barry Henkin August 2014

Dedication

In Memory of
My Mom, Sarah Henkin,
My Dad, Sanford Henkin,
My Sisters, Mardelle and Donna,
and My Friend, Laurie Ripley

Dear Maria
Hope you liked
My Story,
Best wishes
Barry Henkin

Prologue

Barry was born on September 29, 1961, to a middle-aged mother who was unable to care for him. His temporary placement in what was to have become his adoptive home was terminated less than a year later due to concerns about physical and developmental deficits. On August 17, 1962, Barry was placed in foster care with the Henkin family in Shaker Heights, Ohio. He arrived as an infant, listless and unresponsive. His transformation into a devoted son, a loving brother, a loyal friend, and a productive worker is the subject of this book, which has been written in Barry's own words, with a little help from the many friends whose lives he has brightened with his magnanimous spirit.

Introduction

"What makes Barry special? That's actually a very hard question to answer. Barry is special in so many ways that it's nearly impossible to choose one. Overall I would have to say that it is his heart that makes him so special. He is the most caring person I have ever had the pleasure of knowing and my life is all the better for it. Barry cares for everyone, especially his family. His heart is huge and full of kindness, generosity, caring, and love. Ever since I was a little girl I've received a birthday card and a call on June 22nd; never once has he forgotten...He has never made me or my family feel anything less than loved. We love Barry deeply, with all our heart, and we are so thankful to have such a special person be a part of our family."

Hanna Henkin, Cousin

That's me with Delilah. Photo courtesy of Ed Wittenberg.

My name is Barry Henkin. I'm writing this book because I want to help people.

I loved my father and my mother and sisters. They took real good care of me. Now I take care of myself.

I live with my cat, Delilah. Sometimes it's hard. I get lonely. But I have my cousin Scott and his wife Carolyn and their daughter

Hanna. They live in West Sacramento, California. And I have some real good friends.

Lots of good things have happened to me. I won a gold medal in the Special Olympics. I've met lots of famous people. I have a good job. I found out yesterday I'm in the Cleveland Heights High School Distinguished Alumni Hall of Fame! I'm real excited about that. And there's lots more I want to do.

I think you're special too. Like I'm real good at music, and maybe you don't even like music. But everybody's good at something.

This story is how it works for me. I hope you like my book.

******

Chapter 1 – My Family

"I've known Barry since Sarah first took him into her home. He's special in so many ways, and even though he has some challenges, his accomplishments are many…Life can be cruel, but Barry doesn't let it get him down. He thrives on pushing himself forward to let the world know he and others like him can do a lot of things no one ever would have imagined they could achieve."

Marcia Braunstein, Family Friend

My parents, Sarah and Sanford Henkin.

My parents were Sarah and Sanford Henkin. They raised me since I was a baby. They're gone now.

It was my birth brother, Steve, who told me about my birth mother. He's almost 15 years older than me. Steve didn't know he had a brother until he was 13 years old. It was on February 25th 2000, when I came home from bowling at Cedar Center Lanes that I got the call. He lives in Florida. I've never met him. Sometimes I dream about meeting him.

Steve said two of my birth mother's sisters, Anna and Rhoda, lived at Menorah Park Center for Senior Living. That's where I work. I've been there 31 years. I probably knew them and didn't know.

Steve said my birth mother got hit by a car when she was a little girl. She walked with a limp. He said my birth father abused and abandoned her. That's why she couldn't take care of me. She's dead now. She died in June of 1981. She's buried in Tallahassee Florida.

It turns out my sister Mardelle knew my birth mother back in the sixties when Mardelle was working for the Cuyahoga County Welfare. But she never told me. Mardelle was 19 years older than me. I loved my sister. She was real good to me. She died of a diabetic coma on July 6th 2007.

My father, Sanford, has been dead a long time. He was a clerk in the Main Post Office on Public Square. He died in the operating room of Mt. Sinai on December 3rd 1977, of a heart attack. It was my father who told me I would be good working with people. And that's what I did. My father was the greatest man I ever knew.

Mostly I grew up in Cleveland Heights and that's where I went to school. I loved my teachers. Some of them, like Mrs. Stovsky, I still talk to and everything.

On my sixteenth birthday, my father told me to go into the bedroom and there would be something there for me. On my bed, there was a new suit. He said, "I'm gonna call a cab and take you to my favorite restaurant and treat you to a steak dinner and your first beer." He took me downtown to John Q's Steakhouse, and said I could order anything I wanted. That's when I had my first beer. It was a Budweiser. I'll never forget it. Then before dessert came he gave me an envelope with some money in it. It made me feel real special. I miss my father. He was my role model.

My senior Cleveland Heights High School photo, 1980.

My mother, Sarah, died June 15th, 2001. She was real kind. Everybody loved her. She had Alzheimer's and was living at Menorah when she died. Before, when we were living together, I told my sister she was forgetting. I knew something wasn't right, but no one believed me for a long time.

When I give my speeches, sometimes they ask me about my parents. But I don't like to talk about it too much. I miss them.

My other sister Donna was 16 years older than me. I had to convince my sisters to let me live on my own. Bad things happened, but they didn't like to hear about it. But then they believed me. I've been living on my own since 2000. I've lived in this apartment since May 2006. Donna got cancer in her kidney and her breast. She died October 24th 2003.

I have another brother and some nieces and nephews that I don't see no more.

My mother had a brother Bernard and he and his wife, Hilda, had a son David who used to be married to Maureen. Maureen and I keep in touch. Maureen has a sister Deborah and I spend Christmas with her and her daughter Jessica.

My mother's sister Edith was married to Joe and they had a son named David too. David and me kept in touch. He lived in New Mexico with his wife, but he died in 2011. My Aunt Edith had a daughter too, but she stopped talking to me in June of 2000.

Me and my Uncle Herb — I still have that John Lennon shirt!

My father had a brother, Herbert. Uncle Herbert always said I was his favorite nephew. He was real nice. He had a son named Scott with his first wife, my Aunt Margaret. He lives in West Sacramento with his wife, Carolyn, and their daughter, Hanna. I visit them whenever I can. I use my income tax money to take the plane and stay with them for a week. Hanna just graduated from high school and she is going to the University of California, Davis. She has a boyfriend already, and he's real nice too. Scott and his family are the only family I am close with now.

This is my cousin Scott with his wife Carolyn and his daughter Hanna. She's big now.

Chapter 2 – My Job

"We encountered one another for the first time the day I began my brand new career as an occupational therapist...From our very first meeting, Barry was a gentle and calming presence...I wandered into my new department unsure of just about everything that day, and Barry made me feel truly welcome by his genuine warmth and genuine friendliness. Instantly, a potentially difficult and awkward day started out wonderfully. Of the words that can be used to describe Barry, genuine is my favorite...He has a demeanor that is pure, simple, and uncomplicated. He finds joy in all that is around him and that joy can be seen in the twinkle in his eye and in his perpetual smile. He is fun loving but works hard too... And last but not least, Barry is one snappy dresser! I am proud to be counted among the people he calls friend."

Anne Gangidino, OTR, Menorah Park Center for Senior Living

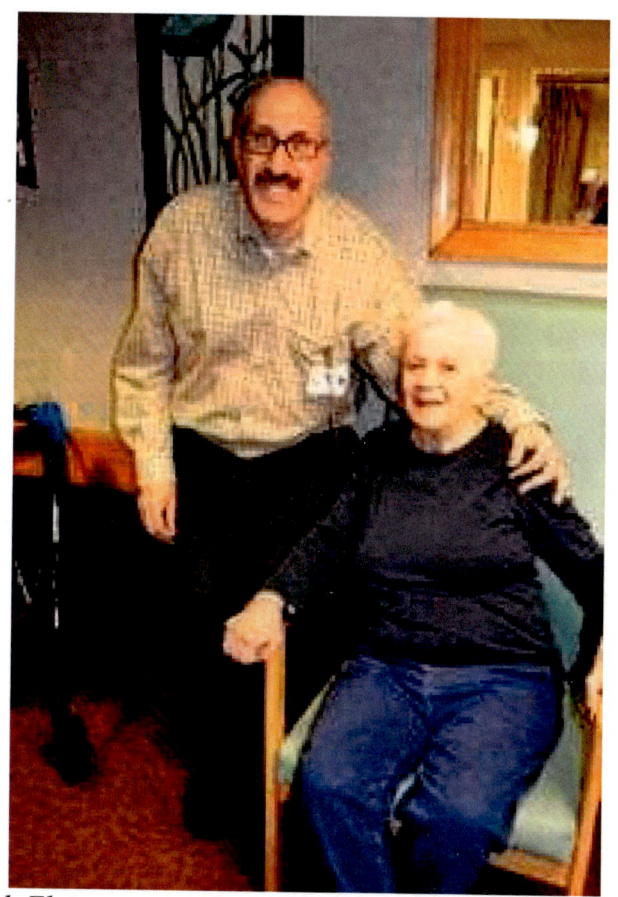

Me with Elain — at work as a Transporter at Menorah Park in Beachwood, Ohio.
Photo courtesy of Sherry Gavanditti.

I love my job.

In April of 1980, just before I finished up at Heights High, I went to a job training program. I had to get up real early and take two buses to get there. I didn't like working there. My boss was real mean. He used to say that his ancestors killed my ancestors in the Holocaust. But I had a crush on the secretary. Her name was Julie and she was beautiful. On break, I used to visit Julie. She used to give me extra bus tickets. She was real nice.

On November 8th at 2 p.m. I was working on the sealing machine and my boss said I was slacking on the job. He swore at me and then he said that thing about the Holocaust. I told him to drop dead and started to walk out. He asked me where I was going. I was shaking like a leaf. He was using real foul language.

I told his boss, Ralph, what happened. He admitted it, and his boss fired him. Ralph told Julie to drive me home.

But I didn't stay there too long. I was only there from April 12th to November 8th 1980. When the day came for me to pick up my last check, I got all dressed up and pretended to be my twin sister coming to pick up my check for me. It was funny. I had no mustache then. I didn't grow my mustache until 1984.

Ralph said he would do his best to help me find another job. And Julie took me out to dinner too.

Then in January 1981, Ralph called to tell me he got me a job interview with Menorah Park. We did not have a lot of money so I went to the thrift store to get a blue-gray sports jacket and navy blue pants. You have to look good when you go for an interview.

They asked me at the interview when I wanted to start. I told them the next day. They said the next day was Friday. I said I didn't care, I wanted to work. At first I was just part-time in the workshop. Then for awhile I was an assistant in the sheltered workshop. Now I'm a transporter in the rehab department! I've been there 32 years! The pay isn't real good but everyone there is real nice.

I get there at seven in the morning. I've got to get there because they need me to help the patients get where they need to go. In the morning, I help deliver the newspapers. And in between transports I help with the shredding. So the day goes fast.

I know everyone there. Not just the patients, but their families who come to visit. When I go out with my friends, I'm always running into someone from Menorah Park. They say, "Hey, Barry," and I ask them how their mother or their grandmother is doing. I remember their birthdays. And if someone dies, I always call the family to offer my condolences. I like people. And I have a real good memory. I never forget a face.

It's a pretty big place so I walk a lot during the day. My boss is real nice. And my co-workers too. Sometimes there is someone, you know, who is mean. But I don't have any problems. It's them that have the problem. That's what I try to remember, and I don't let it bother me. If it's something, you know, more serious, I can always talk with my boss about things, and my friends at work.

My friend Cameron is the one who helped me start writing this book. He doesn't work there now. But we were great friends. People would come from all over the world to visit Cameron, and he would always introduce me to them.

One day, while I was waiting for another resident, there was this lady named Irene there. Irene lived at Menorah Park too. She told me she could tell how much I loved my job. She said I should write a book. That gave me the idea. Then one day I told Cameron about it. Cameron always makes me feel really special. He said Irene was right and that he would help me find a way to do it.

Now one of my friends at work is helping me write this book. My friend Sally who works in the rehab department goes out with me for sushi sometimes. I love sushi. Another friend from work, Melanie, she always picks me up if the snow is real bad so I don't have to wait for the bus. Three times a week she takes me to work so I don't have to take the bus. Sometimes Sherry and some of my other co-workers have me over for dinner or a barbeque.

One of my closest friends at work was a nurse named Laurie. On my 40th birthday, we had a party and she came. She was all dressed up. I joked that I didn't know she had legs because she always wore pants! She told me I was a very good friend and that she wanted to look special for me because I was special. I'll never forget that. One time she invited me to her house for dinner with her and her family. We had roast beef and broccoli and baked potatoes. She reminded me of a singer. She died of breast cancer on September 28th, 2010. She was 46 years old.

A lot of the families of the patients I take care of have become my friends too. And a lot of my friends from school and from camp, now their parents or grandparents live at Menorah Park and we see each other there.

30 years and I still love my job! Photo courtesy of Sherry Gavanditti.

Mark Stovsky has been a real good friend to me. He says I'm like part of his family. We went to camp together and we played on the same team in a basketball league when I was 12 years old. We lost touch for awhile. But then his wife, Shannon, her grandmother came to live at Menorah Park. Mark is like a brother to me now. Mark and Shannon and the kids, I don't know what I'd do without them. I always go to Mark's brother's house for a cookout on the Fourth of July, and sometimes Mark's family invites me over for dinner.

I've won lots of awards for my work. The first one was in 1990. That was for *Employee of the Season*. In 1994, I was *Employee of the Year*. In 1998, I received the *Lena Kaufman Kindness Award*. I got another award, the *Service with a Heart Award*, from Menorah Park in 2003. And when I celebrated my 30th year of service, they threw me a big party.

Barry Henkin - Employee of the Season

When you examine the criteria for achieving the Employee of the Season Award, Barry Henkin is a perfect match. As far as creativity, Barry is socially creative. He finds many ways to work with residents in his job. He is extremely reliable, you can count on him at all times, and he is one of the steadiest performers on the Menorah Park Staff. He takes great initiative, especially in his work on the Employee Activities Committee. His ability to work with others is uncanny, as he is very popular. His attitude towards residents is a model for all. He is caring, friendly, and warm. His attendance is usually perfect. As you visit his department, his loyalty shows, especially when presenting the workshop to a visitor or a job candidate on tour. Barry takes great pride in knowing everyone's name. His leadership qualities are shown in his daily efforts of running the workshop.

5/14/90

MDW/jkm

1990 letter nominating me for Employee of the Season.

Employee of the season
Friendly Barry Henkin honored for compassion, dedication

The Therapeutic Recreation Department, Beauty Shop, and Volunteer Departments named Barry Henkin employee of the season. Mr. Henkin is a therapeutic recreation assistant in the workshop of the home. He has over 9 years of service from what first started out as a part-time job in the workshop.

On May 14, a special luncheon honoring Mr. Henkin was held in the activities center. Staff from all three departments along with Steve Raichilson, Executive Director, and Mark Wisner, Director of Human Resources, joined in the festivities. A surprise visit from his mother, Mrs. Sarah Henkin, and his sister, Mrs. Donna Jurinsky, highlighted the affair.

Barry is most known as an outgoing, friendly individual. He was acknowledged for his dedication and continual display of compassion while working with the residents. Barry is very well known and liked by the staff and seems to know everyone by name.

Employees of the Season receive $50 and have their portrait and name displayed in a special display in the rear lobby of the Center. Recipients are also honored at the following annual spring awards banquet with a certificate significant of the honor.

Barry Henkin, therapeutic recreation assistant, (center) is honored by Nathalie Diener, director, and John Davidson, manager of the therapeutic work center.

November 1990

Article about my award. Courtesy of Menorah Park Employee Newsletter.

Chapter 3 – My Adventures

"We have known Barry for over 35 years, and are so thrilled and proud of his accomplishments. He was our camper when we were counselors at JCC's Anisfield Day Camp. I can still picture little Barry climbing on the bus each morning with his big smile and floppy dark hair. Barry has always been an upbeat person. Even as a child, he had an inner strength that kept him from feeling different. That strength has obviously carried him through life, and made him the positive man he is today. We love spending time with Barry because he is so funny and loves to share stories about the people he meets, his love of music (he could work at the Rock Hall with his vast knowledge!), and his family and friends."

Ellen and Jack Wohl, Long-Time Friends

Me and New York oldies DJ Cousin Brucie from my scrapbook version of the Rock and Roll Hall of Fame. Photo courtesy of Ed Wittenberg.

A lot of time when I speak, people ask me about my hobbies. I have a lot of fun things I like to do.

I love music. You can ask me anything, anything about a record from the sixties, the seventies, the eighties, on up to today. I just remember things.

My best friend, Ed, he takes me to a lot of concerts. I've had a chance to meet a lot of cool people, you know?

The very first person I met was Hank Ballard (his band was The Midnighters and he wrote *The Twist*). I said, "I'm a big fan of yours. Do you mind if I have my picture taken with you, and your autograph?" That's how it all started.

Now I have pictures of me with Joey Dee (remember *The Peppermint Twist?*); Cynthia Lennon (I met her when she was at the Holiday Inn in Independence, July of 1995); and Norman N. Nite (he's a disc jockey on Sirius Radio and I met him at the Rock and Roll Hall of Fame).

I've also got great pictures with Herb Reed of The Platters, Arlene Smith from The Chantels, Mary Wilson of The Supremes, Sonny Geraci (he sang *Precious and Few),* Gary Puckett from Gary Puckett & the Union Gap, Bill Burkette (the lead singer with The Vogues), Jimmy Beaumont from the Skyliners, and Carl Gardner from The Coasters (they were the ones who sang *Charley Brown, Yakety Yak,* and *Poison Ivy).*

You remember Lloyd Price? He sang *Personality*. I really love that song. I also have a picture with Lou Christie. He sang *Lightnin' Strikes* and *Rhapsody in the Rain.* Do you like *Ain't Got No Home?* That was Clarence "Frogman" Henry. I've got pictures with him too. The other ones I have so far are Ronnie Specter of The Ronettes (they sang *Baby I Love You* and *Be My Baby),* and Peter Noone (he was the lead vocalist for Herman's Hermits.)

But my favorite music story I don't have a picture for. I was dating this girl Betty. We were double-dating with this other couple and we went to the movies. They ditched us. It was raining real bad and we didn't know how we were going to get home.

Then I saw this guy, and I asked him "Aren't you Michael Stanley?" And he says, "How do you know who I am?" So we started talking. How do I know? I know every song he sang. He's a great songwriter, you know, and I'm a big fan.

Well, Michael Stanley takes us home and he tells us he'll be playing at Blossom that summer and he wants us both to come. A few months go by, and the night of his concert, this limousine comes to get us and takes us all the way to Blossom for the concert. That was a good night. That was Michael Stanley.

I do other things too. I have a cat. Her name's Delilah. I take care of her.

The year my mother died, I competed in the Special Olympics. I won a Bronze Medal in bowling in 1997. Then, in 2001, I won a Gold Medal in bowling and an award for being the Most Popular Athlete. I dedicated that to my mother because she died that year.

A star in his own right

BOB JACOB Freelance Writer

Barry Henkin will never be mistaken for Shawn Kemp but, in his own way, he is an all-star, too.

Henkin, a member of the Cleveland Heights Special Olympics basketball team, doesn't swish jump shots with relative ease or finish fast breaks with slam dunks like his favorite player. But he does control the rebounds off the glass and connects on most of his patented left-handed short shots.

Henkin, a 36-year-old South Euclid resident, is enjoying his first season of basketball for Paul Ealy's squad. His first game of the season ironically came on the day of the National Basketball Association's All-Star Game, in which Kemp became the first Cleveland Cavalier named to a starting position.

Henkin proved to be an all-star that day, too. In his debut, his scoring, rebounding and passing helped his team defeat the Orange Lions, 35-6. Henkin scored the first points of the game en route to finishing with 10 points to tie for game-scoring honors.

"This is my first time playing basketball (with a team). It is very exciting," says the always-smiling, bespectacled and mustachioed Henkin, who won a silver medal in bowling last year.

Henkin exhibits the same intensity in practice as in games. He's always calling for the ball and, if he doesn't have a shot, he's looking to pass to a teammate. After a good play, he's always looking for someone to high-five. In practice at the Hillcrest YMCA, he wears a Kemp jersey with a big No. 4 on it. He tried to get that jersey, but it was not available in his size.

"Shawn Kemp is my idol," says Henkin. "I like his style of play. I'd like to meet Shawn and have my picture taken with him," says Henkin. "I'll go to see him if I get tickets. That's my biggest wish in the world."

Henkin became a foster child when he was 9 months old.

"I took in a lot of foster children, but I've never had anyone like Barry," says his mother, Sarah. "He has turned out to be perfect." His father, Sanford, died when Barry was 16.

"I have the nicest compliments about Barry," confirms his adoring mom. "He's a great child. He doesn't have a mean bone in his body. He's very giving."

That demeanor has come in handy in his job at Menorah Park Center for the Aging, where he's been a steady employee for 17 years. He works directly with residents as a rehabilitation assistant.

"His very strongest point is his memory of people's names," says Mary Rinas, his supervisor at work. "He never forgets a person once he's met you. He remembers things like birthdays and anniversaries."

Henkin, whose older siblings Jonathon, Howard, Donna and Mardelle, all live in the area, is also a big music fan. He attends a lot of "oldies" concerts with a friend.

Henkin is one of 42 athletes who competes for the Cleveland Heights Special Olympics team, under the direction of Evelyn Reid.

"Barry is really outgoing," she says. "He's really good. He thinks he's Kemp."

And in his own way, Barry Henkin

> "I'd like to meet Shawn Kemp and have my picture taken with him."
> — Barry Henkin, Special Olympics

I like basketball too, but don't get to play it much now. Courtesy of Cleveland Jewish News.

I still bowl every Sunday. I've been in a bowling league since 1984! My previous team gave up on me, but now I play with a team called the Pinheads. I've played with them since 1997. They're good guys. We do pretty good. Our dues are $18 a week. It's a sanctioned league and everything.

*That's me with the Pinheads (Saul, Don, and Mike).
Photo courtesy of Sherry Gavanditti.*

The other thing I like to do is go out to dinner with my friends. I don't drive though. We either go out after work or my friends pick me up. My favorite food is sushi. I write a restaurant review column in the employee newsletter where I work. Every month I try out a different restaurant and offer suggestions to my coworkers.

A couple of times they wrote about me in the papers too. One year, someone nominated me for Person of the Week.

PERSON OF THE WEEK

This University Heights resident is a patient transporter at Menorah Park in Beachwood and has worked there for 28 years.

When he's not wheeling clients and residents to therapy, educational activities or around campus, he can be found working on a book.

His dream is to complete a book for special needs children who don't understand why the world sometimes treats them harshly.

It includes things he wants to share with others about how having special needs doesn't mean having to be treated differently.

Henkin, 47, is a loving and respected person at Menorah Park and is always cheerful, smiling and polite.

He was on the Cleveland Heights Special Olympics basketball team and has won various awards at work, including Employee of the Month and the Lena Kaufman Kindness Award.

He loves listening to Reba McEntire music and hopes to meet her one day.

Barry Henkin

Know someone who qualifies as Person of the Week? Submit nominations at cleveland.com/sun, e-mail them to rjablonski@sunnews.com or mail to Sun Press, 5510 Cloverleaf Parkway, Cleveland, Ohio 44125.

Person of the Week, Courtesy of Sun News.

When I won, Judge Montgomery saw the story and wrote me a real nice letter.

JUDGE K. J. MONTGOMERY
SHAKER HEIGHTS MUNICIPAL COURT

3355 Lee Road, Shaker Heights, Ohio 44120
Telephone (216) 491-1324
Fax (216) 491-1314

September 4, 2009

Mr. Barry Henkin
C/O Menorah Park
27100 Cedar Road
Beachwood, Ohio 44122

Dear Mr. Henkin:

Congratulations on your 'appearance' as the Person of the Week in the *Sun Press!* I read the article and just had to send a quick congratulatory note. If you can still smile and be cheerful after twenty-eight years, you must truly love your job. That's not to mention being a patient and kind individual. Your book sounds quite interesting. It will explain so much to children who are not only challenged by their own needs but by a world that is not always as understanding and patient as it should be.

Again, congratulations and the best of luck with your book!

Sincerely,

K.J. Montgomery, Judge

KJM/wsr

(NOT PRINTED AT TAX PAYERS EXPENSE)

Letter from Judge Montgomery

Another time they wrote an article about me and the Mayor of Beachwood gave me a plaque with the story on it.

The Sun Press
Thursday, January 12, 2006

SNAP SHOT

Barry Henkin

Age: 44
Residence: South Euclid
Occupation: Transporter at Menorah Park
Family: Sister Mardelle Swed, brothers Howard and Jonathon
Hobbies: Bowling, music, concerts, watching sports
Favorite music: '80s and '90s, Reba McEntire
Favorite vacation: West Sacramento, Calif.
Favorite food: Sushi
Favorite movie: "Urban Cowboy"

SUN PHOTO BY JOSEPH DARWAL

He's always smiling

By ED WITTENBERG
Staff Writer

Barry Henkin wears a perpetual smile on his face while working at Menorah Park Center for Senior Living, and co-workers and residents notice.

Friday marked 25 years of employment for Henkin at the Jewish nursing home in Beachwood, and staff surprised him with a cake.

"I love my job," he said. "The people I work with are real supportive of me, and so are the residents and their families.

"Every day I meet a lot of new people. I just like making people happy every day."

Henkin's job at Menorah Park was his first after graduating from Cleveland Heights High School in 1980. He started out in the activities department, but has worked as a transporter in the rehab department since December 1997.

Henkin, who rarely misses a day of work, was named Menorah Park's employee of the year in 1994. His other honors include the Lena Kaufman Kindness Award in 1998 and the Service with a Heart Award in 2003.

"I'd like to meet a nice woman and have a steady relationship," he said when asked about his goals, "someone who drives and has a nice family."

And will he stay at Menorah Park another 25 years?

"Probably so," he responds, with that ever-present smile.

Compliments of
Mayor Merle S. Gorden
City of Beachwood

Snap Shot, courtesy of Sun News.

The last two years I've been practicing public speaking. That's mostly what I'd like to do next.

Chapter 4 – My Challenges

"Barry is a real hero when it comes to dealing with some tough life issues. He is a loyal worker and friend who wakes up each and every morning and decides he is going to make somebody else's day/life better. We need more people like Barry Henkin...The world would be a better place."
Steve Presser, Friend whose Wife's Grandparents were at Menorah Park

Bad things happen to everybody. I remember crying at my sister's grave and wanting to die. I remember lots of things that I don't want to talk about here. There are a few people who have not been nice to me but I don't want them in my book.

When I get depressed, or I have girl problems or something, I call my cousin Carolyn in California. Everybody should have someone like that to talk to.

I have different friends for different things.

My friend Ed gets backstage passes to see musicians. We used to live on the same street and our mothers got us together. My second home is the Rock and Roll Hall of Fame. I visit it with Ed. He's the one I call if I need to go to the post office, and he takes me to the grocery store every two weeks too. The doctor and the dentist are right across the street though, and there are lots of restaurants I can walk to — so things like that I do on my own

Me and my best friend, Ed. Photo courtesy of Sherry Gavanditti.

When I get confused about money or taxes or stuff, I call my friend Linda. She used to work at Menorah Park, and she helps me with my bills too.

If I have an emergency with my cat, I call my friend Debbie.

Winter is the worst, after dark. Then I can't go out much. I'm afraid to take the bus at night. I might get lost or robbed.

But I have lots of friends I talk to on the phone. My teacher, Mrs. Strovsky, sometimes I talk to her. She was an inspiration to me. Then there's Rochelle and Richard. Rochelle's mother was at Menorah. And Brett, sometimes we have dinner together. There's Linda and Jack, and Jack and Ellen. She gets me tickets to see Jim Brickman. She works for him. Thanksgiving and sometimes Easter too, I'm with my cousin Shannon who lives in Dublin, Ohio. Her grandfather and my mother, Sarah, were brother and sister. Jason and Jennie live far away too, but sometimes we get together for dinner.

Then there's my friends from high school. There's Clifford. And Michael. Michael played pro football. He sent me an autographed picture, but I haven't talked to him lately. My friend Tricia I really love. She was so kind to me. She is really special, but she lives far away now. The last time I saw her was at our 10th High School Reunion. Maybe she'll come home for another reunion sometime and I can see her again. That would be really nice.

Chapter 5 – My Goals

"Knowing Barry has motivated me to try to get the most out of my ability, as I know he does. I know that he looks up to me, as kind of a 'big brother,' so I try to set a good example for him, not only when we're together, but when we are apart, as I think of him often. He has inspired me to stick with things when the going gets tough."

Best Friend, Ed Wittenberg

There are still a lot of things I want to do.

I started making motivational speeches when I knew I was going to have my book published. The first time was for Deepwood Center. There were about 15 or 20 people there. And some of my friends came to hear me too. It was fun and everybody was real nice.

Since then, I've talked at a lot of places. The Metzenbaum Center in Geauga County. That's where I met my good friend, Sarah. She's been really good to me and is helping me find ways to make new friends. There was a vocational program in downtown Cleveland where the people were mostly doing farm work. I've been to visit my friend, Broadies Hayes at the Maple Heights Adult Activities Center twice now, with different worker groups. I've been to speak at Beachwood Adult Activity Center twice now too. Sometimes I run into people I knew at camp or school, and there are lots of new people too. Sometimes there are only six or seven people. Sometimes there are 50 or even more.

University Heights man gives motivational speech in Beachwood

Barry Henkin, left, of University Heights, listens to a question during his talk to about 60 clients at the Beachwood Adult Activities Center July 26. Offering assistance is Kevin Coleman, habilitation supervisor at the center. A 1980 graduate of Cleveland Heights High School, Henkin is a transporter in the rehabilitation department at Menorah Park Center for Senior Living in Beachwood, where he has worked for 31 years. He was giving a motivational speech to clients at the center, which is overseen by the Cuyahoga County Board of Developmental Disabilities.

That's my friend, Kevin Coleman, introducing me at the Beachwood Adult Activity Center.
Courtesy of Sun *News.*

What I like to talk about is what you have to do to live on your own, to get a job, to pay your bills, and things like that. I tell them how it's important to look nice and professional when you go on a job interview. A lot of them are working in workshops with other disabled people. But sometimes I think they'd like to be more on their own. So I try to tell them what I learned. How to be kind to people, and if they're not kind to you how it's not your problem.

My first speech! Photo courtesy of Sherry Gavanditti.

I tell them how much I love my job so they know they can find a job they love too. Sometimes they ask me questions. I like to tell them how I spend my day, what I do at work, about Delilah, and about all my friends and the things we do together. I hardly ever miss work, and I tell them how it's important to do your job really good because people are depending on you.

I like when they ask questions. Sometimes they ask me for help finding a job. I can't really do that. But I tell them "You have to do it for yourself. Who do you know? Who can you call? You're special too. There's a job where you'll be happy like I am."

It would be fun to be a coach and help other people so that they could do more things. I could counsel kids with disabilities, and they could call me if they have problems. I'd be there for them.

My dream is to speak at the City Club Forum and even on TV, like on The Ellen Show or with Katie Couric. And to people who have the jobs that would be the kind of jobs it would make people happy to have.

Some of the people I talk to are scared about living alone or going on a job interview. But I tell them if I can do it they can too. It's important to have goals.

There are other things I want to do too. I'd like to meet Reba McEntire. She's my idol. I have 23 of her CDs. My favorite song is "Till You Love Me." When I'm feeling lonely, I imagine someone who feels that way too, and I feel better. I've seen Reba in concert a couple of times. Her music really inspires me.

I'd like to get married someday, to find a nice woman who likes to have fun, is easy to talk to, likes cats, and wants to spend time with me. I was engaged once to a girl named Sue. We met in 1984. But in July of 1986 her mother called the wedding off. Betty, the girl I was dating when we met Michael Stanley, she was seven years older than me, only she didn't tell me at first. That's why I broke it off.

There was only one girl I really cared about. Her name was Karen and we went on a blind date in 1990. I bowled with her father and stepbrother. Her parents picked me up and we went to Mama Santa's. She was a real good girl. We had so much in common. She was so special. We were going to an Indians game, and her Mom called to tell me that Karen had died of a brain hemorrhage.

I'd like to find someone like her. Other people, they lie and hurt other people, and still someone wants to marry them. I can't understand that. I would like to spend my life with someone who wants to spend her life with me.

Epilogue

"Barry has proven that anyone is able to reach his/her goals through hard work and by being a great person in the community. He has shown that even though his strengths and other peoples' strengths might not be the same, he is able to excel in other areas that most people can't."

Josh Kaplow, Friend whose Grandmother was at Menorah Park

I don't use Facebook myself, but my friends will share your posts with me. Photo courtesy of Ed Wittenberg.

There have been times when I thought this book would never be finished. The first writer my friend Cameron introduced me to was too busy to write the book herself so she asked her friend, Sharon, to work on it. Sharon was a nice lady, but she lived far away and then she got real sick and couldn't drive any more. So then the first writer, her name is Joanne, talked to a lady who works at Menorah Park named Sherry. Sherry is my good friend. Sometimes her husband picks me up and I have dinner at their house. While Sherry was working on the book, Joanne helped me find places to speak so I could get used to public speaking. Then, a few months ago, Sherry gave the finished book to Joanne and asked her to change it so it was me and not her speaking. That's the book you are reading now.

I hope you like it because there is a lot more I want to do now that it's finished. I want to speak to as many people as I can about being special and how much you can do if you just try your best and don't let things bother you.

If you would like to join Barry's circle of friends or to have Barry speak at your organization, please visit
www.facebook.com/Barry.Henkin.Fans.